Acting
Out
Luke's
Message

Lenten Dialogues Exploring the Gospel of Luke

Roger E. Timm

CSS Publishing Company, Inc.
Lima, Ohio

ACTING OUT LUKE'S MESSAGE

FIRST EDITION
Copyright © 2015
by CSS Publishing Co., Inc.

For more information about CSS Publishing Company resources, visit our website at www.csspub.com, email us at csr@csspub.com, or call (800) 241-4056.

e-book:
ISBN-13: 978-0-7880-2832-8
ISBN-10: 0-7880-2832-4

ISBN-13: 978-0-7880-2831-1
ISBN-10: 0-7880-2831-6

PRINTED IN USA

Reviews for
Acting Out Luke's Message

Roger Timm has created a wonderful four-set series of Lenten dialogues based on Lucan themes to use in any of a variety of settings including Lenten worship or with Lenten study groups. His dialogues are engaging, thought-provoking, informative and challenging. What would it be like to be a fly on the wall as Luke is struggling to write his gospel account of some parables? How do our life stories intersect with the life stories of biblical characters such as Mary, Zacchaeus, or Cleopas? What do some of the overarching biblical themes mean for us today? What are the untold stories of those whom we commemorate and how does their witness speak to us? These are the themes that run through Timm's dialogues, most of which end with a question to keep the conversation going. This is a great resource for engaging people in thoughtful, faithful reflection and conversation.

Karen Matthias-Long
Associate of the Bishop
Northeastern Pennsylvania Synod/ELCA

*With gratitude
to the people of
St. John's Lutheran Church of Emmaus, Pennsylvania,
and to my grandchildren, Catherine and James Raynock,
for lifting my spirits and enjoying my dialogues.*

Table of Contents

Lenten Commemorations

Introduction

This book includes three series of Lenten dialogues based on the gospel of Luke, intended for use during Cycle C of the Revised Common Lectionary. Working with the assumption that Lent is a time for study and reflection and avoiding a focus on the Passion narrative before Holy Week, I wrote each of these series to explore messages from Luke from several different perspectives.

The first series, *Exploring Parables of Jesus in Luke,* includes five dialogues that focus on parables of Jesus found only in Luke. Since these six parables (I examine two parables in the fifth dialogue) are found only in Luke, I assume that they present important windows into Luke's particular emphases. These dialogues are written as a conversation between Luke and Theophila — or "Thea" for short. Luke dedicates his gospel and the Acts of the Apostles to Theophilus; since I preferred to include both men and women in these dialogues, I took the liberty of changing the name to Theophila.

The second series, *Encountering Characters in Luke's Gospel,* deals with characters who are significant in Luke's gospel, especially as they illustrate important themes that Luke emphasizes. I use "character" to include both actual people in Luke's gospel as well as characters in some of Jesus' parables. The dialogue partners are Lucy and Evan. The names are not essential to the dialogues, but I thought "Lucy" was appropriate for discussing Luke and "Evan" suggests "evangelist," although it is the Welsh form of "John." ("Eva" and "Luke" might serve as well, although having Luke as a dialogue partner might lead to confusion with Luke the gospel.)

The third series is *Lucan Stories in the Gospel and Acts.* The gospel of Luke and the Acts of the Apostles are written by the same author, as indicated by the dedication to Theophilus at the beginning of each book, and they include interesting parallels in theological emphasis. To explore these parallels I imagined a conversation between two characters: Joanna, one of the women who accompanied Jesus and his disciples during his public ministry (see Luke 8:1-3), and Barnabas, a prominent follower of "The Way" who was sent on missionary journeys (first mentioned in Acts 4:36-37).

This book also contains a "bonus" series of Lenten dialogues, *Lenten Commemorations.* Since St. Patrick's Day fell on a Wednesday one year, I decided to depart from my custom of writing dialogues on the gospel for that year's lectionary cycle and instead to write a dialogue series based on commemorations of saints and other exemplars of Christian faith that fell within the five weeks of Lent. The characters in these dialogues are introduced in the narrator's speech at the beginning of each dialogue, but let me add some additional comments. The first dialogue is a conversation between Marcion and Perpetua. Marcion is the author of a second century account of Polycarp's martyrdom. I used the name "Perpetua" because a woman named Perpetua was martyred for her faith about the same time as this dialogue supposedly takes place, but she lived in Carthage, not Ephesus. The characters in the dialogue about Saint Patrick are Sister Fidelma and Brother Eadulf. I borrowed those characters from the Sister Fidelma of Cashel mysteries written by Peter Tremayne, the pseudonym of Peter Berresford Ellis.[1]

These dialogues were used originally within a service of Evening Prayer that was part of a midweek Lenten gathering for a meal and worship. The dialogues could also be used in a Sunday worship service, a retreat setting, an adult forum studying Luke, or for personal study and meditation.

We kept the setting for the dialogues simple — two chairs in front of the congregation, perhaps with a few props suggested by the specific skit. Such simple staging makes these dialogues usable in many contexts, but more elaborate use of props and stage settings may be helpful in reinforcing the message of each dialogue. The conversation in these dialogues is intended to be realistic and to express the good-natured banter that might occur between friends or family members. Dialogue participants should be encouraged to emphasize these moments of humor in the script.

---

1. The occasion of the conversation in my dialogue at the Synod of Whitby is the location of the first of the Sister Fidelma of Cashel mysteries, *Absolution by Murder* (St. Martin's Press, 1995).

Exploring Parables of Jesus in Luke

The Good Samaritan

Luke 10:25-37

Narrator: As he is revising his gospel, Luke is talking with his patron, Theophila, who is underwriting his writing project. He calls her "Thea" for short.

Luke: I've tried to write a more orderly account of the life of our Lord for you, Thea. What do you think of it?

Thea: Your story captures the essence of our faith quite well, Luke, but every now and then Jesus says something that surprises me.

Luke: That's quite true. The disciples talk about how often Jesus surprised and even confused them. But what do you mean?

Thea: Well, I enjoy some of the parables of Jesus that you include in your book. I don't think that brother Mark included them in his gospel.

Luke: No, he didn't.

Thea: I'd like to ask you about some of them. Take, for example, the story about the Samaritan person who stopped to help the man who was beaten by robbers.

Luke: Ah, yes, that's one of my favorite parables. What's surprising about it for you?

Thea: Well, I could have been that lawyer asking Jesus, "What must I do to be saved," and I don't think Jesus answered his question.

Luke: Somehow I've never thought of you as a lawyer. What do you mean, that could have been you?

Thea: I think I've told you why I became a Jew. I grew up worshiping our Greek gods, like Zeus and Athena, but I became disillusioned with all the stories of their immoral exploits. The Jewish belief in one God who calls us to a code of moral behavior was very appealing to me. You know how you've convinced me that Jesus came to fulfill the promises of our one God. So I can imagine asking Jesus how he would describe the expectations our one God has for us.

Luke: In a way Jesus does. He doesn't disagree with the lawyer's answer, "Love the Lord, your God, with all your heart, soul, strength, and mind and love your neighbor as yourself." That is a good summary of what God expects of us.

Thea: Yes, but Jesus never defines what "neighbor" means. Who am I supposed to love? Jesus surprises and confuses me by not answering that question. I'm looking for guidance for my life, and Jesus doesn't give me any here.

Luke: Oh, but he does!

Thea: Where? Instead of listing the people we should love, he tells this little story about two self-centered, unhelpful religious workers and a generous stranger. Didn't you tell me that the Jews and Samaritans hated each other? What kind of twist is this that the Samaritan seems to be the hero of Jesus' story?

Luke: I think Jesus is using this twist in his story to catch our attention and help us to think about the meaning of his parable. But tell me first, do you think the lawyer sincerely wanted an answer to his question?

Thea: I'm not sure, although you did say that he was testing Jesus.

Luke: Right. Jesus seems to sense that the lawyer was less interested in understanding God's will than in limiting the extent of his responsibilities. I think he was hoping for a narrow definition of "neighbor" so he would have a smaller group of people to love. The story has an ironic twist, for usually "neighbor" was defined to include members of one's own people, but here help comes, not from one's own people, but from a stranger from a hated nearby ethnic group.

Thea: That's very nice, but how does that answer the man's question?

Luke: In a way it doesn't, but I think Jesus is suggesting that the man was asking the wrong question, or approaching the question in the wrong way.

Thea: What do you mean?

Luke: The question should be, not "Who is my neighbor?" but "How can I be a neighbor to someone in need?" Jesus thinks the lawyer is trying to narrow down what he needs to pay attention to; Jesus wants him to be open to noticing people in need, whoever and wherever they are.

Thea: Are you saying that I should not be looking to Jesus for some description of the moral code I should follow every day?

Luke: No, you shouldn't, if that moral code might serve to limit your response to people who need to know God's love for them.

Thea: What should I be looking to Jesus for?

Luke: Jesus doesn't give us a moral code as much as he teaches us what kind of attitude to have as the basis of our moral code. Jesus says, "Look for opportunities to show neighbor love regardless of who the person is."

Thea: You still haven't defined "neighbor" for me!

Luke: That's on purpose. Our neighbor can be anyone we encounter who has some need for our love and compassion.

Thea: You're saying that the parable may call on me to love someone who is not my neighbor in any sense? Does Jesus expect me to love someone who is not a relative, nor a person who lives near me, nor someone from my own social class or circle of friends?

Luke: Yes! Again, Jesus told that lawyer to be less concerned about who his neighbor is and to be more ready to be a neighbor to whomever we meet with need for help.

Thea: This Jesus you tell about is not only surprising but just plain difficult to follow!

Luke: How true, how true! But remember how difficult it has been for him to love all of us.

Thea: You're right, Luke. How moving it was to read how even when he was suffering the painful death of crucifixion, he died with words of forgiveness on his lips. He showed this love of neighbors even to the soldiers who crucified him and the criminals who died with him.

Luke: Yes, Jesus showed us what to do by the way he loved others — and loves us still.

The Rich Fool

Luke 12:13-21

Narrator: Luke is talking with his patron, Theophila, whom he calls "Thea," as he sits in her seaside villa in Ephesus, working on his next book, *The Acts of the Apostles.*

Luke: Thea, I surely appreciate your invitation to use your home to begin work on my second book about how the good news of our Lord Jesus spread from Jerusalem all across the empire to Rome.

Thea: Brother Luke, I'm happy if I can help you. Your story of our Lord's life and resurrection helped me understand him so much better that I'm glad to help with the next step in your writing.

Luke: Thank you. Sitting here and hearing the sounds of the seaport and smelling the sea breeze stimulates my thinking and brings back memories of the times I sailed with Brother Paul on his trips to share "The Way" with people who had not yet heard of Jesus.

Thea: Usually my husband and I find this house quite satisfying too.

Luke: Usually?

Thea: Well, yes. Lately we've been thinking that the house is not big enough for us.

Luke: Not big enough? It seems quite spacious to me.

Thea: Perhaps it seems that way to you, but my husband has been quite successful as a merchant here in Ephesus, and he needs more room to store his merchandise. We've been talking about tearing the house down and building a larger one.

Luke: Thea, you did read my gospel, right?

Thea: Yes, Luke, I did!

Luke: Do you remember Jesus' story about the rich man who built larger barns because he had grown more crops than he had room for?

Thea: Yes, I do.

Luke: Does our conversation remind you of that story?

Thea: Not really. We're not farmers, you know!

Luke: Yes, you're not farmers, but you just talked about doing the exact same thing as the rich man did in the story.

Thea: I suppose you're right, but that reminds me. I've been meaning to speak with you about your attitude about rich people. You seem quite content to enjoy our seaside villa; yet you emphasize much criticism that Jesus directed toward wealthy people. Is that fair? Besides, the rich man was expressing the view I've heard from the scriptures that material well-being is a blessing from God, and several places encourage us to eat, drink, and be merry — and praise God too. What's wrong with the rich man's attitude?

Luke: I must have touched a nerve! I'm glad you said something to me if this has been troubling you. Jesus' story is not directed to everyone who happens to be rich. First of all, the rich man had come to believe that his wealth was due to his own skill. His building bigger barns was an expression of his confidence that he was in control of his life and the source of his success.

Thea: What arrogance! We don't feel that way, Luke. We thank God for whatever success we've had, and we know that we can depend only on God for what makes our lives truly rich and rewarding.

Luke: I'm glad to hear that. Notice also how Jesus says, "Be on your guard against all kinds of greed, for one's life does not consist in the abundance of possessions." Jesus is not speaking against all wealth; Jesus is warning against greed and against a kind of idolatry that sees life's ultimate goal as acquiring possessions.

Thea: So do you think our talk about building a larger villa reflects such greed or idolatry?

Luke: Ordinarily I wouldn't think so. I know how deep your faith in Christ is, and I've seen how generous you have been, not only with me, but also with our poorer brothers and sisters here in Ephesus. But when you began to talk about your plans, they sounded so similar to the plans of the rich man in Jesus' story, that I had a momentary fear that you were giving in to a temptation to be greedy.

Thea: I can see why you thought that, Luke, and your questioning our reasons for rebuilding is a helpful reminder for us to reexamine our reasons for our plans. So far when we've talked about it, our reasons are purely practical. We need more space for our business. We don't see our business success as the central value of our lives. We long to be united with our Lord Jesus, and meanwhile we are happy that we can share what God has given us with others who need our help. We think life consists in sharing our blessings, not in accumulating more and more of them.

Luke: I'm glad to hear that, Thea. I'm sorry if I jumped to the wrong conclusion in comparing you with the rich man in Jesus' parable.

Thea: That's all right, Luke. I do think my husband and I need to consider whether the parable applies to us or not. But I do have another question.

Luke: What's that?

Thea: Did Jesus ever tell a story with a rich man as the hero?

Luke: Hmmm. There's Zacchaeus...

Thea: Right! The corrupt tax collector who extorted money out of innocent common people. A great positive model of a wealthy person!

Luke: He did repent and make amends! He promised to give half of his wealth to poor people and to give back four times what he may have taken illegally from people. And then there's Joseph of Arimathea who let the women bury Jesus in his tomb.

Thea: A better example.

Luke: Oh, yes, there's the Parable of the Dishonest Manager.

Thea: That doesn't sound so positive.

Luke: It is in Jesus' own peculiar way — but can we talk more after I've written a few more chapters?

Thea: Of course. Come down to the atrium later so that we can "eat, drink, and be merry"!

The Dishonest Manager

Luke 16:1-13

Narrator: Luke is talking with his patron, Theophila, whom he calls "Thea." They are continuing a conversation they have been having about the parables of Jesus that Luke has included in his gospel.

Thea: I'm glad you mentioned the parable about the dishonest manager, for this is the one parable that my husband and I have the most difficulty with. Jesus seems to be approving dishonesty and even theft. As I told you before, I became a follower of Christ because I thought his way encouraged moral behavior. What about this parable? If my husband catches one of his managers misappropriating funds, is he supposed to commend him?

Luke: It seems that way, doesn't it? The parable, though, doesn't really tell us for sure that the manager was stealing from his master. He was "squandering" the master's money; he was spending the master's money excessively, not stealing it. When he told the master's debtors to change what they owed his master, that may have been a kind of theft, but he may have been taking off his own commission in order to gain favor with the customer so that he might have a job after his master fired him.

Thea: Hmmm. So the manager may not have been quite as dishonest as he seems at first. Yet the parable seems to be commending him for behavior that is more questionable than moral. He still seems shady to me.

Luke: He is shady, I suppose, but Jesus often said things that were shocking or outrageous to get people to think carefully about what he said. Remember how he said, "It is easier for a camel to go through the eye of a needle than for a rich person to get into the kingdom of God."

Thea: Another example of a negative attitude toward rich people, by the way, but I agree that the image was shocking. I still laugh at the picture in my mind of a camel getting stuck in a needle between its humps.

Luke: I think Jesus is trying to surprise us with this parable too. But notice that he doesn't commend the manager for his ethics; he commends him for being clever. This shady manager reacts to his personal crisis in a way so clever that his master is impressed, even if he disapproves of what he did. Jesus is saying that as we face crises in our life of faith, we should be just as clever in figuring out what to do about them.

Thea: I haven't usually associated cleverness with faith. I thought we were supposed to be as innocent as children.

Luke: As *trusting* as children, but that doesn't mean we need to be naive or thoughtless as believers. Jesus realized that his message about God and his claims about himself caused a crisis of faith for those who heard him. Jesus wants to encourage his disciples to be thoughtful and clever in how they respond to him.

Thea: We should be thoughtful and clever, even if what we do is a little shady?

Luke: No, Jesus doesn't mean that. Again, the parable may seem to suggest that, but it is part of the way Jesus uses exaggeration to get us to think about how we live out our faith.

Thea: So this parable has to do with being clever in expressing our faith and has nothing to do with money?

Luke: Not exactly; it's more complicated than that.

Thea: That shouldn't surprise me, I guess.

Luke: Jesus commends the manager for being shrewd in how he used his master's money. Part of what he means is that we should be shrewd in how we use money. Just as the manager used money to curry favor with potential employers, we should use money to please God. If we use money in ways that please God, then that will be a sign that we will seek to please God in other ways too.

Thea: Is this just another way for you to get my husband and me to give you more money for your collection for poor believers here and in Judea?

Luke: Do I seem that crass? My answer is "yes" and "no." I do think that contributing to our collection for the poor is a way to use our money in a way that pleases God, but that's not the only way. You might think of other ways too. In my next book I'll give several examples of how the first followers of our risen Lord shared their possessions in common so that those who needed help would receive it.

Thea: So the clever way to use money is to give it away?

Luke: Partly that's true, but you have to use some to take care of your family and maintain your business. Beyond that we can be creative and thoughtful about how to share the money and wealth God has given us with people in need. Every Christian may have different opportunities for such sharing.

Thea: Actually, I can think of many needs right here in Ephesus.

Luke: I think it will be good if the parable helps you to think about how to help with those needs. The main thing that Jesus warns against is turning money into another god. Mammon can be simply the finances we need to support life, or it can become a god we worship instead of our Lord.

Thea: I see that in some of our business partners, Luke. All they live for is to accumulate more and more wealth. They hardly have any time for their families or friends, and they don't even enjoy the things they have. Yes, Jesus is right — it is important to be clever about how we use the money we have.

Luke: I'm glad you see the message of Jesus' parable so clearly, Thea.

Thea: Do you think you could have written it more clearly in the first place?

Luke: I don't think so. The power of the parable is in its mystery.

The Rich Man and Lazarus

Luke 16:19-31

Narrator: Luke is talking with his patron, Theophila, or Thea, while he is working on his next book, *The Acts of the Apostles.*

Thea: How long do you think it will take you to finish your book about the apostles?

Luke: I'm almost done. I'm writing now about Paul's final journey, the time he came to Rome and was able to witness to the gospel in the capital of the empire.

Thea: I'm glad that I can help you finish your writing project. I'm eager to see how many people will believe in Jesus as their Lord after they hear your story about Jesus' death and rising again, plus your new book about what amazing things the apostles did once they realized that Jesus was risen.

Luke: Don't forget the role of the Holy Spirit!

Thea: Right. The disciples would never have found the courage to share their faith without the help of the Holy Spirit.

Luke: Thea, I appreciate your enthusiasm for my writing, but I don't have the same confidence that people will automatically believe in Jesus just because they hear the story of his death and resurrection.

Thea: You don't? Why not? Your sharing the story of the resurrection persuaded me to see Jesus as the fulfillment of God's promises.

27

Luke: Do you remember the time I went along with Paul the first time he went to Greece? Paul went on to Athens, and he talked about the resurrection with a gathering of philosophers in their central marketplace. They all dismissed him, probably thinking he was crazy.

Thea: Well, he was talking with philosophers — they always doubt everything!

Luke: All right, but think even of the end of my gospel. After Jesus had been raised from the dead, he was talking with two of his disciples as they were walking to their home in the village of Emmaus. Even after Jesus explained how what had happened to him was anticipated in Moses and the prophets, they didn't believe him or even recognize him — until he broke bread with them.

Thea: This reminds me of Jesus' parable about the rich man and Lazarus. Didn't the rich man want Lazarus to go and warn the rich man's brothers about how awful Hades was?

Luke: Right. And Father Abraham refused, for he said that his brothers had Moses and the prophets. When the rich man argued that someone risen from the dead would persuade them, Abraham replied that if they didn't listen to Moses and the prophets, they wouldn't listen to a risen person either.

Thea: How ironic that statement is! You surely have shown that the witness of the risen Jesus did not automatically compel people to believe in him. Why do you suppose that's true?

Luke: I think people won't hear the message about Jesus if they're not open to the Holy Spirit touching their hearts and if they have other loyalties that interfere with believing in Jesus.

Thea: What do you mean?

Luke: Consider the rich man. He lived a very extravagant, self-centered lifestyle. He wore expensive clothes and feasted every day, not just once in a while. He didn't even pay attention to poor Lazarus on his doorstep. If he had truly listened to Moses and the prophets, he would have heard how important it is for believers to help the poor and hungry. The rich man was so committed to his own comfortable, extravagant lifestyle that he couldn't hear God's call to feed the poor person at his gate.

Thea: I couldn't believe how arrogant that rich man was! Here he ignored Lazarus in his earthly life and then he is brazen enough to ask Father Abraham to send Lazarus like a servant with some water.

Luke: That did take some gall!

Thea: That parable reminds me of one of Jesus' sermons where he says, "Blessed are you who are poor, for you will receive the kingdom of God," and then he added a little later, "Woe to you who are rich, for you have already received your reward."

Luke: I'm surprised that you're not complaining again about how a rich person is portrayed in this parable.

Thea: I've given up on winning that battle, Luke. Besides, you have shown me a helpful way to understand Jesus' teaching about wealth.

Luke: What's that, Thea?

Thea: The trouble with the rich man in this parable is not that he is rich. The trouble is that he is so wrapped up in his own pleasures that he ignores the Bible's clear command to care for people in need, and he turns a blind eye to Lazarus, whose needs are obvious right at his gate.

Luke: Right. This parable leaves us with two questions.

Thea: It does? What are they?

Luke: What message is the Holy Spirit speaking to us through God's word right now?

Thea: That's an important question, and we have even less of an excuse not to hear the Spirit's message than did the rich man.

Luke: Why do you say that?

Thea: Because not only do we have Moses and the prophets in the scriptures but we also have Jesus risen from the dead — plus new writings like the letters of Paul and your gospel.

Luke: That's right, and if we open our hearts and minds the Spirit will show us God's will for us.

Thea: And what's the second question?

Luke: Are there opportunities for helping people in need that we are missing because we are so focused on ourselves that we can't see them?

Thea: That's an important question too. These parables of Jesus that you write about have helped me see that Jesus came to show us God's love and that following Jesus means to think not just about ourselves but also to open our hearts to share God's love with others around us.

Luke: Then there will be no Lazarus lying at the gate of your villa!

Thea: I should hope not! I appreciate these good questions you raise. They should give me something to think about while you finish writing!

Week Five

The Widow and the Unjust Judge
and
The Pharisee and the Tax Collector

Luke 18:1-14

Narrator: Luke and his patron, Theophila, or Thea, are talking on a Sunday afternoon while she is preparing to host the house church that meets in her home every Sunday evening.

Thea: As I've been reading your gospel, Luke, I keep noticing how often women play an important role in your stories. Usually women remain more in the background in our society. Was that different in Galilee?

Luke: No, that was true in Galilee too, but Jesus was different. The twelve disciples were all men, but women followed Jesus too — Mary Magdalene and Joanna and Mary, the mother of James, one of the disciples. It was those women who helped with Jesus' burial and went to the empty tomb on the Sunday morning our Lord rose.

Thea: Jesus seemed to care especially about widows. He restored life to the son of the widow from Nain, and he showed concern about the widow who put her last coin in the treasury in the temple.

Luke: Well, our scriptures do command us to pay special attention to widows and orphans, partly because they have no one else to take care of them.

Thea: I especially enjoyed the story of the widow who was so persistent in pursuing her court case that she totally annoyed her judge and persuaded him to rule in her favor so that he would be relieved from her nagging. I applaud her courage and gutsiness!

Luke: And well you should, but do you remember the point of Jesus' parable about this feisty widow?

Thea: The point wasn't to encourage women to be feisty?

Luke: I fear I may be getting in trouble with you, but, no, that wasn't exactly the point.

Thea: What was it then?

Luke: Jesus was teaching us about prayer. His point was that God invites us to pray with as much persistence and determination as the widow approached the judge. If a judge who admittedly neither fears God nor respects other people will grant this widow's request, how much more will our compassionate God hear our prayers!

Thea: I liked this widow's gutsiness, but I did think that she was a little impolite, almost rude even. Shouldn't we be polite and courteous when we pray to God?

Luke: It isn't wrong to be polite and courteous, but God does invite us to be honest in our prayers. Some of our psalms express upset and anger with God, and our patriarch Jacob even wrestled with God until God gave him a blessing.

Thea: I appreciate that encouragement to share how we really feel in our prayers. Now about that widow again — it doesn't matter that it's a woman in the story?

Luke: It does matter somewhat. It's another example of how Jesus came to turn our expectations upside down. This widow, a person who doesn't count for much in society, is the example of the persistence that God responds to.

Thea: Whether or not it's important that a widow is the main character in Jesus' parable, it is important that we pray persistently.

Luke: Exactly! One thing I tried to show in my gospel is how often during his ministry Jesus stopped to pray.

Thea: But not any kind of prayer will do.

Luke: I suppose not, Thea, but what do you mean?

Thea: Well, right after the story about the widow Jesus tells the parable about the Pharisee and the tax collector. Jesus didn't seem to like the Pharisee's prayer.

Luke: No, he didn't.

Thea: Why not?

Luke: What he said was more an expression of pride than of prayer. The Pharisee in the parable wasn't praying to express his concerns to God or to acknowledge his need for God. Instead he was describing how wonderful he thought he was.

Thea: So is it wrong to thank God for the blessings in our lives? During our prayer time in our love feast tonight I was going to thank God for the privilege of hosting our house church in our home. Is that any different than the Pharisee's prayer?

Luke: I agree that we have to beware of spiritual pride too. God doesn't appreciate our being thankful for how wonderful we are. But that's different than being genuinely thankful for the good things God blesses us with. Which kind of prayer would your prayer be?

Thea: I'm not planning to thank God for how wonderful we are! We do feel sincerely privileged to host our house church here. I don't think there's anything special about us or that we've done something to deserve this privilege.

Luke: If that's true, then your prayer of thanksgiving sounds acceptable to me. Jesus' parable is another way of showing how God turns things upside down. Ordinarily we would expect a pious Pharisee to please God and a corrupt tax collector to be rejected. But God operates differently than we expect. God doesn't judge our prayer by our social status or wealth or position in the church; rather God looks for repentance, humility, and a genuine reaching out to God because we recognize how much we need God.

Thea: Now I'm wondering if I have to be careful about how I pray.

Luke: Why do you say that?

Thea: It seems as if I'll need to be careful not to pray like that Pharisee in the parable but like that tax collector instead.

Luke: If you mean thoughtful when you say careful you're right, but not if you mean hesitant to pray. Remember how persistently the widow approached the judge. God wants prayer to be a constant part of our life of faith. God invites us to have an on-going conversation, letting God continually know our hopes, fears, joys, and needs.

Thea: Jesus did say that God appreciates determination in prayer.

Luke: Yes, Jesus' parables encourage us to be persistent, genuine, and humble in our prayers.

Thea: Thank you, Luke. I'll be able to pray more freely tonight. Don't forget to join us for our fellowship meal.

Luke: I'll be there. I just have to finish my last chapter about Brother Paul reaching Rome.

Encountering Characters in Luke's Gospel

Mary, the Mother of Our Lord

Luke 1:26-56 (or 46-56)

Narrator: Lucy and Evan participate in a Bible class at their church and have agreed to read through the gospel of Luke as part of their Lenten discipline, paying special attention to the characters they encounter in his gospel. Their conversation begins just after they finished reading the story of Jesus' birth in the opening chapters of Luke.

Lucy: It seems strange to be reading the Christmas story during Lent.

Evan: So you don't think shepherds and angels fit the spirit of the Lenten season?

Lucy: I don't. Reading it reminds me more of Christmas pageants than Holy Week and Easter celebration.

Evan: I can understand why you say that, but the chapters about the births of Jesus and John the Baptist set up some of the themes Luke will emphasize later in his gospel.

Lucy: Are you saying that these chapters are like a prologue to the rest of the gospel?

Evan: Yes, I think so.

Lucy: That makes sense. I was impressed with what we learn about Mary in the first two chapters. She really was a special person.

Evan: A "special person"? That's quite an understatement! She's only the blessed Virgin Mary, the Mother of our Lord!

Lucy: Okay, maybe "special person" doesn't adequately describe her, but I mean something other than what we've come to say about her. I know that we honor her as the mother of our Lord, but reading these chapters again impressed me with some other things.

Evan: What other things, Lucy?

Lucy: For one thing, we may give her great honor now, but then she was a lowly, humble person. People think she was young, barely a woman, and she was from Nazareth — an unimportant town in the backwater territory of Galilee. She was no princess in some castle in Jerusalem.

Evan: An unlikely person to be the mother of our Lord?

Lucy: It seems that way to me.

Evan: I think you're right, but that's a common theme that runs through the Bible. God often works through people you wouldn't expect. Jacob was a schemer who cheated his brother out of his birthright. Moses killed someone and escaped to the desert before he came back to lead the people of Israel out of Egypt. The mighty King David grew up as a lowly shepherd boy. God often surprises us by working through unlikely people.

Lucy: So God works even through you?

Evan: Hey, don't use my words against me! But that's right — and God can work even through you too!

Lucy: Touché! But I agree. Mary is someone of humble status, but there's something else that impressed me.

Evan: What was that?

Lucy: I was impressed with how willing she was to accept what God was asking of her. She replied to the angel by saying, "Here am I, the servant of the Lord. Let it be with me according to your word."

Evan: Is that so impressive? Wouldn't you respond that way if you encountered an angel coming to you like that?

Lucy: I don't know. I hope I would. Mostly I think I'd be scared to death. But many people in the Bible resisted God's call. Moses said he wasn't good at public speaking, Jeremiah said he was too young, and Jonah hopped on board a ship and went the opposite direction from where God wanted him to go. I think one of the special things about Mary is how willing she was to be God's servant.

Evan: She is someone to admire for being open to following God's call. I suppose that's something we can try to imitate.

Lucy: Yes, it is. But there's still more.

Evan: What else?

Lucy: I've heard and sung the song Mary sang for Elizabeth many times, but its message really struck me this time.

Evan: What about it?

Lucy: Mary sees God's calling her to be a sign of whom God favors. God scatters the proud and lifts up the lowly. God fills the hungry with good things and sends the rich away empty. That seems pretty radical.

Evan: It does, and we often think that wealth and positions of power are blessings from God.

Lucy: We do, and maybe they are, but I think Mary's song has a warning for us.

Evan: What kind of warning?

Lucy: I think when we have blessings of wealth or power, we become proud, think we have accomplished something completely by ourselves, and forget about recognizing our need for God.

Evan: So God favors the poor and lowly because they recognize their need for God?

Lucy: I think that's what Mary is saying.

Evan: Do you think we should become poor and lowly so that God will favor us?

Lucy: No, I don't think that! I do think we should remember our need for God whatever status we have in life. Mary's song can remind us of the humble attitude God favors.

Evan: I think that Mary's song also encourages us to share God's concern for the poor and hungry. We can find ways to fill the hungry with good things too.

Lucy: Right. Reading the story of Jesus' birth in Lent may seem strange, but it's helped me see some important messages for my faith. Besides honoring Mary as the mother of our Lord, we can honor her too for her willingness to obey God's will for her.

Evan: We can also honor her as another example of how God works through people we wouldn't expect to be special servants of God. We can join her in praising God for favoring the poor and needy.

Lucy: There's more.

Evan: Isn't that enough?

Lucy: No, because I think it is important for us to ask ourselves, "How can and does God work through me, even if I don't expect that God could use me to carry out God's will?"

Evan: And one more question: "What can we do to show that God cares for the poor and hungry?"

Lucy: (*turning to the congregation*) What does encountering Mary mean for you?

Week Two

The Sinful Woman and Zacchaeus

Luke 7:36-50 (with Luke 19:1-10)

Narrator: Lucy and Evan continue to read through the gospel of Luke as part of their Lenten discipline, paying special attention to the characters they encounter in his gospel. They pick up their conversation as they are preparing for one of the meals offered by their congregation.

Lucy: Have you ever wondered why we have so many meals at church?

Evan: Not particularly. I just like to eat good food, so I come to most of the meals we have. But why wonder why we have meals at church? Isn't a natural thing for groups of people to have meals together?

Lucy: I suppose so. Fellowship is important for churches, and what better way to have fellowship than to gather together for a meal?

Evan: Right. Now does that satisfy your curiosity?

Lucy: Not completely. I see in Luke's gospel that sharing meals with people is important for Jesus. In fact he became known for eating with tax collectors and sinners. Do we have lots of meals because that's what Jesus did, or just to have fellowship together?

Evan: I suspect that we have our fellowship meals just because we enjoy eating together, but it might be good to think about whether we should follow Jesus' example and make a point of eating with the tax collectors and sinners of our day.

Lucy: Jesus definitely used his table fellowship to demonstrate his reaching out to all people, even those not welcome in the polite society of his day.

Evan: He seems to have upset some people because of the kind of people he associated with. Maybe the opposition he experienced had its root in his dining practices.

Lucy: It upset some, but it also touched the hearts of others who came to know a kind of welcome they hadn't known before. They may have thought God didn't care about them, but Jesus showed that God did care by sharing meals with them. I think the sinful woman who washed Jesus' feet when he was eating with Simon the Pharisee is an example of someone like that.

Evan: But we don't know that Jesus shared a meal with her. She wasn't an invited guest at Simon's dinner.

Lucy: Oh, don't be picky! Yes, you're right; we don't know if she had been a guest at a meal with Jesus. But she definitely was one of those sinners he was criticized for sharing meals with. We don't know what kind of sinner she was, but she clearly had a widely known reputation for being one. Jesus' welcome for her, sinner that she was, touched her so deeply that in her gratitude she washed his feet with her tears and anointed his feet with oil, showing Jesus loving signs of hospitality that his host Simon had neglected to perform.

Evan: She certainly was deeply grateful for the acceptance Jesus showed her, and the story is moving when

Jesus affirms the message of God's forgiveness for her.

Lucy: Reading about this sinful woman reassures me that I can count on God's forgiveness too.

Evan: Yes, it does. It also reminds me of another story in Luke's gospel.

Lucy: Which one is that?

Evan: The story about Zacchaeus, who was a chief tax collector.

Lucy: Didn't he climb a tree to see Jesus?

Evan: Yes, he was so short that he couldn't see Jesus over the crowds lining the road where Jesus was walking.

Lucy: Why was he so eager to see Jesus?

Evan: I imagine it was because of all the reasons we've been talking about. He probably had heard that Jesus ate with tax collectors, even though most people despised them.

Lucy: I don't understand that. Nobody likes paying taxes, but we don't despise IRS agents — they're just doing their job.

Evan: Well, some people may despise them, but things were different then. The tax collectors were seen as collaborators with the hated Romans, and they tended to extort more money from people than they owed. Anyway Jesus told Zacchaeus to come down from his tree, for he would be eating with him at his house that day.

Lucy: This story is another example of Jesus' custom of eating with tax collectors and sinners.

Evan: Exactly. One more time when Jesus demonstrated that God's welcome is wide enough to include even people like Zacchaeus.

Lucy: Was he as grateful as the sinful woman who washed Jesus' feet with her tears?

Evan: I don't think he cried over Jesus' feet, but he was definitely grateful. He promised to give half of his wealth to the poor, and if he had defrauded anyone he would pay them back four times what he had taken from them illegally. The acceptance Jesus showed him surely touched his heart and prompted a grateful response.

Lucy: These characters in Luke's gospel — both the sinful woman and Zacchaeus — are touching reminders to me of how wide and deep God's love is. I find comfort knowing that God welcomes sinners like them — and like you, Evan.

Evan: Wait a minute! What do you mean, "sinners like me"? I'm not some awful sinner.

Lucy: You're not? Are you sure you're not hiding something from me?

Evan: No, I'm not hiding anything from you, at least not anything too awful.

Lucy: I believe you, but I could have said "a sinner like me." We may not be as disreputable as either of these two characters, but none of us follow God's will perfectly. And like them, knowing God's welcome for sinners can prompt a grateful response from us too.

Evan: Yes, it can. What kind of grateful response can we have? What might we do that's like washing Jesus' feet with tears and anointing them with oil or giving half of our wealth to the poor?

Lucy: That's a good question to think about. One answer might bring us back to why we have meals. Maybe we could show our gratitude by offering meals that will include the tax collectors and sinners of our day.

Evan: An interesting idea!

Lucy: (*turning to the congregation*) What does encountering the sinful woman —

Evan: (*also turning to the congregation*) or encountering Zacchaeus —

Lucy and Evan: mean for you?

The Persistent Friend

Luke 11:1-13

Narrator: Lucy and Evan continue to read through the gospel of Luke as part of their Lenten discipline, paying special attention to the characters they encounter in his gospel. They just read the verses where Jesus taught the disciples the Lord's Prayer.

Evan: Can you imagine a friend of yours pounding on your door at midnight to ask for some loaves of bread? That seems pretty inconsiderate.

Lucy: Actually I can. I had a friend who did that once.

Evan: Really? At midnight? Weren't there any grocery markets or convenience stores open that they could have gone to?

Lucy: Well, she wasn't asking for bread and she wasn't pounding on my door. But she did call me at 2:00 in the morning and ask me to get some medicine for her.

Evan: Why did she do that? Couldn't she have taken care of that during the daytime?

Lucy: She was in a panic. Her husband was out of town, and one of her children had developed a high fever and wasn't able to sleep. She didn't know what to do.

Evan: How did you react to her phone call?

Lucy: At first I was pretty groggy to be awakened so early in the morning. Then I was annoyed to be disturbed in the middle of my beauty sleep. At first I said I couldn't help her. I told her that I had to get a good night's sleep because I had an important presentation to make at work that morning.

Evan: Did that get you off the hook?

Lucy: No, she kept on asking because she felt desperate. She doesn't have any family around here, and I'm her closest friend.

Evan: So what did you do?

Lucy: I finally agreed because she seemed so desperate and was so persistent.

Evan: How did your presentation go the next morning?

Lucy: It went fine. It's amazing what a lot of caffeine can do for you.

Evan: Did you get her the medicine she wanted, or did you get a cheaper discount version?

Lucy: What kind of friend do you think I am? Of course I bought what she asked for.

Evan: Just checking! I know how you like to save money and use coupons.

Lucy: So you think I'm cheap?

Evan: No, I'd say frugal. But I was just thinking about how Jesus asked if you'd give a child a snake if they asked for a fish.

Lucy: I noticed that too. I've known some children who would prefer a snake, but, no, I got what my friend wanted.

Evan: So did you feel god-like?

Lucy: You are filled with crazy questions! What do you mean by that?

Evan: Well, doesn't Jesus compare the friend who is tucked in for the night and doesn't want to give his friend some bread with God?

Lucy: I guess so, but in a back-handed kind of way. Remember that he says, "If you who are evil know how to give good gifts to your children, how much more will your heavenly Father give the Holy Spirit to those who ask him!" You could just as well have asked me if I felt like an evil person giving good gifts to my friend.

Evan: Okay, are you an evil person who still can give good gifts?

Lucy: Enough with the crazy questions! I did have mixed feelings about helping out. Like I said, at first I felt annoyed and imposed upon by that 2:00 a.m. call.

Evan: It seems like for you and for the friend in the story persistence was the key. The persistence of the friend ultimately won the helpful response.

Lucy: Yes, my friend's persistence was a key part of what motivated me to respond.

Evan: So Jesus seems to be encouraging us to be persistent in prayer.

Lucy: I think that's right, but I wonder — is persistence in prayer enough?

Evan: What do you mean?

Lucy: Can we be sure that if we persist in prayer God will answer our prayer?

Evan: Jesus did say, "Ask and it will be given you, seek and you will find, knock and the door will be opened for you."

Lucy: Yes, he did say that, but there have been times when I prayed fervently for something and I didn't receive it.

Evan: Fervently and persistently too?

Lucy: Yes, both fervently and persistently.

Evan: God may answer our prayers by saying "No" or by leading us in a different direction. You might have answered your friend's nighttime call, for example, by coming over to watch her kids while she went out or by bringing some medicine that you had in your house or by suggesting someone else to help. Besides, Jesus says that God answers prayer in another way.

Lucy: How is that?

Evan: Remember how you quoted Jesus when he said that God will give the Holy Spirit to all who ask? Maybe the persistent prayer that is promised an answer is a persistent prayer for the Holy Spirit to be with us.

Lucy: So I can't expect God to help me win the lottery if I pray long and hard enough?

Evan: Only if you promise to give 10% to church! No, I don't think you can expect that kind of help. What I think God really hopes for by encouraging persistent prayer is for us to have an on-going, perpetual relationship with God, maintained through our persistence in prayer. Jesus is promising that our openness to God will be filled with the presence of the Holy Spirit with us.

Lucy: Encountering the persistent friend in the story, then, encourages us to be persistent in our prayer life.

Evan: And Jesus encourages this persistence because God wants us to have an ongoing relationship with God.

Lucy: And this ongoing relationship, maintained by persistent prayer, doesn't necessarily mean we'll have whatever we want from God, but it does mean that the Holy Spirit will be a constant presence with us to help and guide us.

Evan: Right! (*turning to the congregation*) What does encountering the persistent friend mean for you?

The Prodigal Son

Luke 15:1-2, 11-32

Narrator: Lucy and Evan continue to read through the gospel of Luke as part of their Lenten discipline, paying special attention to the characters they encounter in his gospel. They just read the chapter that includes Jesus' parable about the prodigal son.

Lucy: The parable Jesus tells about the prodigal son is quite amazing to me. I find it difficult to imagine that a son would do that to his father — demand his inheritance as if the father were already dead and then go off to some place far removed from his family.

Evan: I don't find that difficult to imagine at all!

Lucy: You say that so emphatically. Have you had a similar experience?

Evan: Yes, I have. My younger brother is a drug addict who left home several years ago. We would never hear from him except when he ran out of money. He regularly called my father to ask for financial help.

Lucy: Did your father help him?

Evan: Yes. Even though we were pretty sure my brother was using the money to support his drug habit, my father sent him money. Until recently, that is.

Lucy: Until recently? What happened?

Evan: Well, my father finally woke up and realized that giving him money was only enabling my brother's addiction. The last time my brother called, my father said he wouldn't send him any more money but he could come home and live with us as long as he entered a treatment program for his addiction.

Lucy: What happened then?

Evan: Much to my surprise, he agreed.

Lucy: Really? I guess that was a surprise. How have things been going?

Evan: Okay, I guess. He's in a treatment program and seems to be drug-free. My father is very happy to have his son back, but I'm skeptical about his keeping clean.

Lucy: Your story does sound like Jesus' parable. Your family situation sounds pretty complicated, and I think the parable is more complicated than we usually think.

Evan: What do you mean?

Lucy: Well, the parable is usually called "The Prodigal Son," but I think it could just as well be called "The Resentful Brother" or "The Forgiving Father."

Evan: I can see that, and the point of the parable might be different depending on which title we choose.

Lucy: Exactly. For example, if we choose the traditional title, "The Prodigal Son," we might emphasize how the younger son dishonored his father and also wasted his inheritance, but then when he was at his lowest point he repented and decided to go home and reconcile with his father.

Evan: Is that what you think happened?

Lucy: Yes, don't you?

Evan: No! I think the younger son remained a schemer and manipulator and decided to put on an act of repentance so that he could get more help from his father.

Lucy: You are skeptical, aren't you? What if we chose the title, "The Forgiving Father"?

Evan: The father surely was forgiving. He didn't even wait for the younger son to get all the way home before he ran out to welcome him. Some might think that the father was embarrassing himself to greet his wayward son that way.

Lucy: And notice that he welcomed him even before the son finished the statement of repentance he had practiced.

Evan: Notice also that he treated the older brother in a similar way. When the older brother refused to come in for the celebration, the father went out to plead with him to join in the rejoicing over his brother's return.

Lucy: Right. So if we assume that the father represents God, then the parable emphasizes how amazing God's love is and how far God is willing to go to forgive us, even beyond any ordinary expectations we might have of the limits of God's love.

Evan: I think the parable suggests that we make a mistake if we place limits around God's love and forgiveness.

Lucy: I agree, but let's not forget the third title, "The Resentful Brother."

Evan: I'm not sure I want to think about that one. It might hit too close to home.

Lucy: Do you think so? Might you be like "the resentful brother"?

Evan: Well, I do find it difficult to identify with the joy my father feels about my brother's coming home, although I can understand why he feels that way. I just hope that my brother is sincere and not about to break my father's heart again.

Lucy: Perhaps you share some similarity with that older brother, but notice too that the older brother didn't appreciate how the father cared for him all the time he stayed at home. He felt more like a slave than a favored son. Not only could he not join his father in rejoicing at his brother's return, but he also failed to appreciate the love his father always had — and still would have — for him.

Evan: You know, I think the best title is "The Forgiving Father," because I think Jesus wants us to know how amazing God's love is. God's forgiveness is fuller and deeper than we can imagine.

Lucy: I won't argue with that. If we look at the story from the younger son's point of view, the message for us is that we can be sure that God seeks to welcome and forgive us, even if we don't feel the least bit worthy of God's love.

Evan: And if we look at it from the older son's point of view, the message is not only that we can count on God's love for us, but that God encourages us — even pleads with us — to accept and welcome others, even if we are sure they're not worthy.

Lucy: That can be a challenge for us who are long-time church members, for we can be tempted to resent God's welcome for people who haven't been as faithful and hard-working as we have been.

Evan: Encountering the characters in this parable, especially the forgiving father, assures us of how forgiving our God is and encourages us to join in God's yearning to welcome sinners.

Lucy: Yes, it does. (*turning to the congregation*) What does encountering the forgiving father mean for you?

The Disciples on the Road to Emmaus

Luke 24:13-35

Narrator: Lucy and Evan have finished reading through the gospel of Luke as part of their Lenten discipline, paying special attention to the characters they encounter in his gospel. They are talking during the fellowship time at their church on Palm Sunday.

Lucy: When we began reading Luke five weeks ago, I thought it seemed funny to be reading the Christmas story during Lent.

Evan: But we learned a lot by reading about Mary, didn't we?

Lucy: Yes, we did, but now I also felt like we were getting ahead of the story by reading Luke's accounts of Jesus' resurrection before this Lenten season is over.

Evan: I thought about that too, but we don't forget about the resurrection during Lent. After all, Sundays, even in Lent, are celebrations of the resurrection.

Lucy: You're right. Besides, I felt that encountering the two disciples on the road to Emmaus was definitely a Lenten experience.

Evan: Why do you say that? They encountered the risen Christ.

Lucy: But they didn't know it at first. They were confused about what the women from their group had experienced that morning, and they were still dealing with their grief and sorrow over Jesus' crucifixion. That's about how I feel during Lent — sorrow over what happened to Jesus and confusion about what it all means for me now.

Evan: You put that very well. I can identify with those two disciples too. Our celebration of Easter next week will be very happy, singing all those upbeat Easter hymns, but I think we forget how confusing and even scary that first Easter was for the disciples. They didn't know what to think about what was happening. Was it real? Was it all a vision or a hallucination? Seeing the men in dazzling white was more eerie and frightening than comforting.

Lucy: I could put myself in the shoes of those two disciples, walking on the road to the Emmaus of my faith journey. By the way, why do you think only one of them is named?

Evan: Good question. Maybe because Cleopas was well known among the first followers of Jesus. Maybe because the second disciple was his wife and women didn't count enough to be named.

Lucy: Wait a minute! Women did count, especially in Luke's gospel, but even though Luke does name a number of women in his gospel, I do admit that you might be right.

Evan: The story raises another question for me. Why didn't they recognize Jesus?

Lucy: Maybe the risen Jesus looked different.

Evan: Perhaps. I also know that sometimes when I'm not expecting to see someone at a particular time or place I don't recognize them when I run into them.

Lucy: Yes, that could be. Besides, it says that their eyes were kept from recognizing him. Maybe it was important for them to go through the whole encounter before they realized it was Jesus.

Evan: Yes, I was wondering too why they would be kept from recognizing Jesus, but whatever the reason the whole encounter did have a powerful impact on them.

Lucy: That time while he walked with them on the road to Emmaus gave Jesus the chance to explain how the scriptures referred to him and what he came to do.

Evan: I guess "Moses and the prophets" refers to what was their Bible then.

Lucy: Yes, I believe so.

Evan: I would have liked to hear how Jesus interpreted the scriptures. How inspiring that must have been!

Lucy: Apparently. Later they recalled how their hearts were "burning" while Jesus opened up the scriptures for them.

Evan: I think I know how they felt. I feel a kind of excitement when a sermon or a passage from scripture really strikes home for me, especially when it speaks to something that has been bothering me.

Lucy: You get excited? You usually seem so calm to me.

Evan: Yes, I can be excited when I hear something that inspires me, even if I look calm to you. If I were with those two disciples, I think I would have been really excited when we finally recognized Jesus.

Lucy: Notice that they recognized him at their evening meal, and here we are at our fellowship time sharing food together. Do we have another example of how important meals are for us Christians?

Evan: In a way, but when Luke writes that Jesus took the bread, blessed and broke it, then gave it to them, I think he has a particular meal in mind.

Lucy: Are you talking about the Last Supper?

Evan: Yes, I am.

Lucy: Well, if these two disciples were in that upper room with Jesus, I can understand that Jesus' blessing and breaking the bread would remind them of the last supper with Jesus and open their eyes to who he was.

Evan: Yes, and I imagine that Luke wants us to think of that special meal Christians share — Holy Communion — where we remember Jesus and recognize his presence among us.

Lucy: This all reinforces my feeling that encountering the two disciples on the road to Emmaus was truly a Lenten experience.

Evan: What do you mean?

Lucy: I said before that I can identify with their sadness over Jesus' death and their confusion about what it all means. But now I can see that I also identify with them in how important, even exciting, the explaining of the meaning of scripture can be. Reading carefully through Luke's gospel this Lent has really deepened my understanding of Jesus and his message.

Evan: I agree with that, and I would add that encountering these two disciples has strengthened my appreciation of the importance of Communion. I'll think of them as I recognize the presence of Jesus in the "breaking of the bread."

Lucy: We could turn this around and say that this story is about our encounter with Jesus. We also encounter Jesus in our reading and study of scripture and in our receiving Holy Communion.

Evan: Like those two disciples, encountering Jesus in scripture and Communion encourages us in our faith as we travel on the roads to the Emmauses of our lives.

Lucy: (*turning to the congregation*) What does encountering the disciples on the road to Emmaus mean for you?

Evan: (*also turning to the congregation*) And what does encountering the risen Christ mean for you?

Lucan Stories in the
Gospel and Acts

What Does the Coming of the Holy Spirit Mean for Us Now?

Luke 3:21-22 and Acts 2:1-4 (or 2:1-21)

Narrator: We hear this evening a conversation between Barnabas and Joanna. Barnabas was a prominent follower of "The Way," the name the first followers of Jesus used for themselves. Barnabas, whose name means "son of encouragement," was sent on missionary journeys, sometimes with Paul, from the church in Antioch. Joanna was one of the women who accompanied Jesus and his disciples during his public ministry. Since her husband, Chuza, was the steward of Herod Antipas, the ruler over Galilee, they lived in Tiberias where Herod had made his capital. Barnabas stopped to visit Joanna in Tiberias on his way to visit the church in Jerusalem.

Joanna: Welcome, Brother Barnabas! What brings you to Tiberias?

Barnabas: I'm on my way to Jerusalem to tell our fellow followers of The Way what has been happening in Antioch and on some of my missionary journeys. Since my journey brings me through Tiberias, I thought that I would stop and visit with you.

Joanna: I'm glad you've stopped to visit. I don't think I've seen you since I came back here to Tiberias after those special days when the Holy Spirit came upon us on that Pentecost festival just after our Lord's resurrection.

Barnabas: Those were special days. Sometimes I've wished that I could have been with you and the disciples from the very beginning and experienced the Holy Spirit giving you the gift to speak in all the languages of the people in Jerusalem for the Pentecost festival.

Joanna: That was an exciting experience, but the Spirit has continued to work among us — perhaps in less dramatic ways, but still in powerful ways.

Barnabas: You're right, and I've been privileged to see many of those ways that the Spirit has been at work among us.

Joanna: When have you sensed the presence of the Holy Spirit among us?

Barnabas: There were so many times. I surely felt his power among us when we first began to grow as followers of The Way, and many of our leaders were filled with the Spirit. We sensed the guidance of the Spirit as we lived together in a sharing community and cared for the needs of all our people. Even though he was martyred, Stephen was a Spirit-filled person, and so was Philip when he was sent to share the good news about our Lord with the eunuch from Ethiopia.

Joanna: Have you sensed the Spirit at work, then, among the followers of The Way to guide and encourage them?

Barnabas: Yes, but not only then. Sometimes the Spirit has worked outside our community to push and tug us in the direction God's Spirit wishes for us.

Joanna: Are you saying that you're not always ready and willing to follow the Spirit's wishes?

Barnabas: Don't be nasty to me — but, yes, we've not always recognized what the Spirit wanted us to do.

Joanna: When did something like this happen?

Barnabas: Well, Peter didn't expect to be called to preach the good news about our Lord to Gentiles, but when he went to the house of the Roman centurion Cornelius and shared our message about Jesus, the Holy Spirit came upon Cornelius and his whole household. Later when Paul and I approached the leaders of the church in Jerusalem about not requiring Gentile followers of The Way to be circumcised, we all felt that the Spirit was guiding us to change what we expected and to accept Gentile believers without circumcision. "It seemed good to us and to the Holy Spirit" we said as we reported our decision to our fellow believers in Antioch.

Joanna: So sometimes the Holy Spirit works within and among us, and sometimes the Spirit pushes and guides us in directions we don't expect.

Barnabas: Exactly. The Spirit's presence can be both encouraging and challenging.

Joanna: That was true during Jesus' lifetime too.

Barnabas: Really? How was that?

Joanna: In many ways. For example, we heard that after Jesus was baptized by John the Baptist and was praying, the Holy Spirit came upon him like a dove and then the voice from heaven said,

"You are my beloved Son; with you I am well pleased."

Barnabas: That was surely encouraging to Jesus and all who heard it.

Joanna: Yes, but next the Spirit led him into the wilderness where he was tempted by the devil.

Barnabas: That temptation experience was definitely more challenging than encouraging.

Joanna: Yes, and then came his first sermon in his hometown of Nazareth. On the one hand, Jesus said that the words of Isaiah, "The Spirit of the Lord is upon me because he has anointed me to preach good news to the poor," applied to him. These words were encouraging to us who began to follow him. On the other hand, as he criticized the people of Nazareth for not really accepting him and his message from Isaiah, they became angry with him, hometown boy or not. The Spirit's message in Jesus' mouth was challenging to these people from his hometown.

Barnabas: Yes, the message of the Spirit is not always comfortable or convenient.

Joanna: That's true, but mostly I find Jesus' words about the Holy Spirit encouraging.

Barnabas: I think you're right.

Joanna: You ought to since you are the "son of encouragement"!

Barnabas: Yes, that is what my name means, but why do you emphasize the Spirit as encouraging?

Joanna: I remember when Jesus taught us his special prayer. Afterward he encouraged us to be persistent in prayer and said that God will always give us the blessing of the Holy Spirit when we ask.

Barnabas: That's an important promise that I surely have relied on, especially when I've traveled on my missionary journeys.

Joanna: We have been blessed with experiencing the Spirit at work in Jesus and now with us followers of The Way. Do you think we will continue to see the guidance and support of the Holy Spirit?

Barnabas: I believe so.

Joanna: I surely hope so.

Barnabas: But we need to be careful.

Joanna: Why do you say that?

Barnabas: Because of what we've experienced so far. Like I said, the Spirit's presence can be both encouraging and challenging. Sometimes the Spirit will be a comfort for us; sometimes the Spirit may lead us in ways that are anything but comfortable.

Joanna: So we pray for the presence of the Holy Spirit — and we expect surprises.

Barnabas: Yes, indeed!

What Does Christ's Healing Mean for Us Now?

Luke 13:10-17 and Acts 3:1-10

Narrator: Barnabas and Joanna are continuing their conversation in Joanna's home in Tiberias. Joanna was one of the women who accompanied Jesus and his disciples during his public ministry, and Barnabas, a prominent follower of "The Way" whose name means "son of encouragement," was sent on missionary journeys, sometimes with Paul, from the church in Antioch. He stopped on his way to visit the church in Jerusalem.

Barnabas: Sometimes I wish, Joanna, that I had been able to accompany Jesus during the time he was teaching people while he was in Galilee and then on his way to Jerusalem.

Joanna: Those were special times that I shall always treasure.

Barnabas: What do you remember most from those times when you were with Jesus?

Joanna: That's difficult to say because I see now how full of meaning everything was that he said and did. I suppose how he healed people seems most memorable to me.

Barnabas: Do any particular times of healing stand out for you?

Joanna: There were so many, but he especially seemed to care about women and anyone whose illness separated them from their community. Of course, he healed Mary Magdalene, who was one of us women who accompanied him. I remember the crippled woman in the synagogue, whom he healed on the sabbath. Of course, that healing didn't make everyone happy, because some people thought that he shouldn't heal people on the sabbath. But we thought he was doing God's work, since Jesus freed both Mary and this woman from evil spirits.

Barnabas: You said Jesus seemed to care especially about women. I remember the story of how he restored life to the son of a widow not far from here in Nain. I imagine that she would have been quite destitute with no husband or son to support her.

Joanna: And not just women. I remember when he healed ten lepers. Before they were healed, they had to live separated from their families and community.

Barnabas: What surprised me about that story is that only the one Samaritan leper came back to thank Jesus.

Joanna: Yes, that was a surprise, but often it seemed that the people who appreciated Jesus the most were the ones who felt most distant from God. You know, Jesus' healing reminded me of the healing done by our great prophets, Elijah and Elisha. Elijah raised the son of the widow of Zarephath, and Elisha cured the Syrian general Naaman of his leprosy. People who saw what Jesus did felt that God was at work among us again.

Barnabas: And we know that they are right, for we recognize now that Jesus is God's Son! I think it is a blessing for us that the healing power of our Lord continues among us. Both Peter and Paul healed men who were crippled so that they could walk again. I was with Paul when he healed the man, and the people there thought that God was at work among them.

Joanna: Really? How did you know that?

Barnabas: Actually, it was somewhat embarrassing. They thought I was Zeus and Paul was the god Hermes. We had to insist that we were not divine but that we were the vehicles of the healing power of Christ.

Joanna: It stretches the imagination to think that someone would identify you as divine!

Barnabas: Now is it that hard to imagine?

Joanna: Yes, it is, but I do acknowledge that you are a faithful servant of our Lord. I have also heard about Peter bringing Dorcas back to life over in Joppa. She was such an important leader in the church there that they were at a loss over how to continue without her. Peter's restoring her to life not only restored her to her community but also restored her faithful ministry to them.

Barnabas: Another example of Christ's healing power through us touching the life of a woman.

Joanna: Yes, she was especially important to the widows in Joppa. Barnabas, do you think all this healing will continue?

Barnabas: Yes, I do, but I don't know how exactly. I know that not every sick person will be healed and not every dead person will be restored to life.

Joanna: I know that too, but I wonder what kind of healing we can continue to expect.

Barnabas: You know, I think it's important to look beyond the individual cases of healing and to see what the healing means.

Joanna: As I think about the healing stories we've talked about, it seems that in most cases part of what the healing meant was that people were restored to community. Their illness, their death meant that they were separated from their families and their community.

Barnabas: Right — I think that we can expect that the healing power of Christ will continue to overcome things that separate us from one another. After all, after his resurrection Jesus greeted us disciples with a greeting of peace.

Joanna: Don't forget what the disciples sang when Jesus entered Jerusalem that last week — "Peace in heaven," and when we say "peace," or "shalom," we mean peace and health and being surrounded by a caring community.

Barnabas: What else did these healing stories tell us?

Joanna: Well, that God is among us.

Barnabas: Right!

Joanna: Just as long as you don't think that means you!

Barnabas: Thanks for keeping me humble, but part of what we have felt in these times of healing is that God is at work through us.

Joanna: So what we can expect is that God will continue to be present among us, touching us with the healing power of God's Spirit. Whatever problems we face, we can be sure that we are not alone and that God walks by our side.

Barnabas: Exactly. God's healing will continue among us, drawing us together in caring community and accompanying us through whatever difficulties we have to deal with. Isn't that comforting?

Joanna: Yes, oh "son of encouragement," it is comforting indeed!

What Does God's Care for the Poor Mean for Us Now?

Luke 6:20-26 and Acts 4:32-37

Narrator: Barnabas and Joanna are continuing their conversation in Joanna's home in Tiberias. Joanna was one of the women who accompanied Jesus and his disciples during his public ministry, and Barnabas, a prominent follower of "The Way," was sent on missionary journeys, sometimes with Paul, from the church in Antioch. He stopped on his way to visit the church in Jerusalem.

Joanna: Do you ever wish, Barnabas, that our community could have stayed the same as it was in those first weeks after the Holy Spirit came over us on that Pentecost Sunday?

Barnabas: That was a special time, but we couldn't remain the same and still spread the good news about our risen Lord. What about that time are you thinking about?

Joanna: I remember how at first we shared all our possessions in common. No one was in need, because whoever had a need was given help from what we had together. Didn't you sell some property you owned and give it to the apostles to share with the community?

Barnabas: Yes, I did, and I was glad to do it. In those days we were trying to live a new life that was following the kind of love and compassion that our risen Lord had demonstrated for us.

Joanna: Those were exciting times. You could almost feel the Spirit guiding us in following what Jesus had taught us.

Barnabas: Did Jesus teach you about sharing your possessions with people in need?

Joanna: Not in so many words, but he often talked about God's care for the poor and he warned the rich about their attachment to their money. He said that he came to bring good news to the poor. In one of his special sermons Jesus taught us that the poor are blessed and belong to the kingdom of God, but he warned the rich that they had already received their reward.

Barnabas: That reminds me of Jesus' story about the rich man and Lazarus, the poor, sick man who lay outside the rich man's gate hoping for some scraps of food but never receiving any help from him. After they died, Lazarus was carried by angels to be with Abraham and the rich man was tormented in Hades.

Joanna: Mary, the mother of our Lord, shared with us similar thoughts from the song she sang before Jesus was born — "God has filled the hungry with good things, but the rich he has sent away empty." I wonder sometimes if we can welcome rich people into our community.

Barnabas: I hope so! I don't consider myself rich, but I did own some property. I think it depends on the attitude that rich people have toward God and their money.

Joanna: In Jesus' story about the rich man and Lazarus, the problem with the rich man wasn't so much that he was rich but that he was so absorbed in his money and wealthy life that he didn't even notice Lazarus needing food at his gate.

Barnabas: And don't forget that not everything was completely rosy in those first weeks of our community in Jerusalem. Remember Ananias and Sapphira who sold some property. They kept some of the proceeds but lied to the apostles and claimed they had given it all to them. They died because keeping some of the money was more important to them than being truthful to the Holy Spirit and the apostles.

Joanna: So being rich isn't the problem; being rich and caring about your money more than God or people in need is the problem.

Barnabas: Yes, the question is "Do you worship God or your money?" Or, "Do you care more about yourself and growing your own wealth or about sharing your money with people in need?"

Joanna: I don't think you answered my question, Barnabas.

Barnabas: What question was that?

Joanna: My question about if you ever wish that our churches were like our community in those first weeks after the coming of the Holy Spirit on that Pentecost festival.

Barnabas: Oh, that question! You know, I have mixed feelings about that.

Joanna:	Really? Why?
Barnabas:	Well, on the one hand, that sharing community was really a special experience of living out the kind of love that Jesus showed. I certainly grew deeply in my relationships with God and with the other believers. On the other hand, I don't think we could maintain that kind of community for a long time.
Joanna:	Why not?
Barnabas:	Partly because of how difficult it was for us mere mortals. I mentioned the incident with Ananias and Sapphira. We also had a dispute about whether all people in need were being treated fairly between the Greek-speaking and Hebrew-speaking members of our community. We worked that out, but that showed how difficult living in such a sharing community can be.
Joanna:	Since you worked it out, why not work on maintaining such a sharing community?
Barnabas:	Another reason is that the Spirit led us in another direction. We felt the call to move beyond that sharing community to travel beyond Jerusalem and Judea to spread the message of our Lord all across our world, even to Rome.
Joanna:	Why not set up sharing communities wherever you brought Jesus' message?
Barnabas:	A good question, I suppose, and maybe it could have worked out that way. I see that first sharing community as an ideal and a model for us to follow. However we do it, our responsibility as followers of The Way is to be sure that we care for people in need and to share our wealth

to help them. That's why our brother Paul gathered contributions from churches he founded to help people here affected by that famine.

Joanna: I do miss that close sharing we had in the beginning, but I see your reasons for it not continuing. Besides, I know that our church here does find ways to care for people in need. I guess there are many ways to show that Jesus came to bring good news to the poor.

Barnabas: Yes, and we can continue to ask ourselves, "Do we worship God or our money?" Or, "Do we care more about ourselves and growing our own wealth or about sharing our money with people in need?"

What Does Christ's Forgiving Spirit Mean for Us Now?

Luke 23:32-43 and Acts 7:54-60

Narrator: Barnabas and Joanna are continuing their conversation in Joanna's home in Tiberias. Joanna was one of the women who witnessed Jesus' crucifixion, and Barnabas, a prominent follower of "The Way," was among the first believers in the early Jerusalem community. He stopped on his way to visit the church in Jerusalem.

Barnabas: You asked me if I wished that our community had remained the same as it was those first weeks after the Spirit came over us at the Pentecost festival. Yes, there were things about that time that were especially inspiring, but we had difficulties and challenges too.

Joanna: I know. You mentioned some of the disagreements among us.

Barnabas: Not only the problems within our community. We also faced opposition from people around us who didn't share our faith in Jesus as our Messiah and Lord. I remember that awful time when Stephen, one of our first deacons, was stoned to death because of his testimony about Jesus.

Joanna: That was a sad and frightening time.

Barnabas: It was, but Stephen made quite an impressive confession of faith as the crowd was getting more and more angry with him. He began by describing his vision of Jesus as the Son of Man at the right hand of God. Then when they began stoning him he prayed, "Lord Jesus, receive my spirit," and as he died he added, "Lord, do not hold this sin against them."

Joanna: Stephen's forgiving spirit surely was amazing.

Barnabas: Yes, it was.

Joanna: It reminded me of how Jesus died on the cross.

Barnabas: You were there, weren't you?

Joanna: Yes, I was there with some of the other women who had been accompanying Jesus and his disciples. Yes, we women were there, but not the men who followed Jesus.

Barnabas: Yes, I know; that was not a proud moment for the disciples. But what about Stephen's death reminded you of Jesus' crucifixion?

Joanna: Obviously it was also a sad and frightening time. We had become so close to Jesus that to see him suffer such a painful death was almost too much for us to bear.

Barnabas: I'm sure that must have been very difficult for you.

Joanna: Yes, it was, but that's not really the most important part of Jesus' crucifixion that I was thinking of.

Barnabas: What was it then?

Joanna: Jesus' forgiving spirit as he was crucified was also so amazing.

Barnabas: How did Jesus express that forgiving spirit?

Joanna: First of all, as the soldiers were putting him on the cross, Jesus also prayed, "Father, forgive them, for they do not know what they're doing."

Barnabas: That is truly surprising. Ordinarily you would expect someone being crucified to scream out in pain, or curse out the soldiers crucifying him.

Joanna: Not Jesus. Yes, he obviously was in pain, but he expressed the loving forgiveness he lived by all his life. But that's not all.

Barnabas: What else was there?

Joanna: While Jesus was hanging on the cross, some of the leaders of the people and the soldiers mocked and ridiculed him, adding insult to injury. One of the two criminals crucified with him added his own mockery. Then something else surprising happened — the other criminal defended Jesus and then asked him, "Jesus, remember me when you come into your kingdom."

Barnabas: How did Jesus answer him?

Joanna: Once again Jesus showed his forgiving spirit. He said, "Truly I tell you, today you will be with me in paradise." Jesus was forgiving to the end. Then he was almost calm and peaceful as he died. Like Stephen, Jesus prayed, "Father, into your hands I commend my spirit."

Barnabas: At peace with God, forgiving to people. A wonderful example, but difficult to follow.

Joanna: I remember the challenging words Jesus preached once: "Love your enemies, bless those who curse you, pray for those who mistreat you."

Barnabas: That's so different than our natural impulse to seek revenge.

Joanna: You know, I find Jesus' words and example both challenging and comforting.

Barnabas: I can recognize how what he said would be challenging, but how is it comforting?

Joanna: Oh "son of encouragement," you should see the comfort in Jesus' words! I'm comforted because I can be sure that Jesus will reach out with forgiveness even to me.

Barnabas: You're right, I should not be surprised that you find comfort in what Jesus preached in his lifetime and said from the cross. I do try often to comfort new believers with the assurance of Jesus' forgiving spirit. You also said his words are challenging. I agree; how do you see them as challenging?

Joanna: I find it difficult to forgive someone even if they say they're sorry. Both Jesus and Stephen asked for forgiveness for the people putting them to death even though they weren't in the least bit sorry for what they were doing.

Barnabas: I agree that forgiving someone does seem more satisfying somehow if they are repentant, but I do think that Jesus and then Stephen are trying to move beyond our normal desire to seek revenge. In a way they're leaving it up to God to respond to the evil they're going through.

Joanna: So when we are forgiving like Jesus, we're turning over any response or revenge to God?

Barnabas: That's what I think. But being forgiving doesn't mean denying that we're being hurt or sinned against. Stephen did say, "Do not hold their *sin* against them."

Joanna: Forgiving someone can be both honest and merciful.

Barnabas: What do you mean by that?

Joanna: When I forgive someone, I don't have to be dishonest and say that they didn't really hurt me or sin against me, but following what Jesus taught us by his words and deeds does mean being merciful towards that person who sinned against me.

Barnabas: Yes, and we do it because we are comforted in the knowledge that Jesus loves and forgives us.

Joanna: Just as we continue to pray, "Forgive us our sins, as we forgive those indebted to us."

Barnabas: Amen!

Week Five

What Does Christ's Innocence Mean for Us Now?

Luke 23:44-49 and Acts 26:24-32

Narrator: Barnabas and Joanna are continuing their conversation in Joanna's home in Tiberias. Joanna was one of the women who witnessed Jesus' crucifixion and went to the tomb on Easter morning, and Barnabas, a prominent follower of "The Way," was sent on missionary journeys, sometimes with the Apostle Paul, from the church in Antioch. He stopped on his way to visit the church in Jerusalem, and they had just been talking about what Joanna had seen when Jesus was crucified.

Joanna: When Jesus died, of course we were very sad and upset, and a lot of the people watching were showing their grief too. What really surprised us, though, was what the Roman centurion said when he saw how Jesus died.

Barnabas: What did he say?

Joanna: He said, "Certainly this man was righteous." I think he meant that Jesus seemed innocent to him and not deserving of such a death penalty.

Barnabas: I wonder if he meant something more than that. I wonder if he recognized something special in what Jesus said from the cross and how he died with a prayer on his lips.

87

Joanna: Possibly. Perhaps he saw in Jesus not only an innocent man but also a genuinely righteous person. I wonder if he might be one of those Gentiles who might become followers of The Way.

Barnabas: Well, we know that Cornelius was a centurion over in Caesarea who became a follower of the Way and was baptized by the apostle Peter. Speaking about apostles, when you talk about the innocence of Jesus I am reminded of another apostle.

Joanna: Which apostle do you mean?

Barnabas: The apostle Paul.

Joanna: How does the innocence of Jesus remind you of Paul? I've heard stories about the difficulties Paul faced, and I recall that he was imprisoned on several occasions. Also, didn't you have a disagreement and parting of the ways? How innocent was Paul?

Barnabas: Yes, Paul and I had our disagreements, especially about my cousin Mark. Paul was upset that Mark left us on one of our missionary journeys, but they have reconciled their differences now. And, yes, Paul was imprisoned on several occasions but never for any legitimate reason. So I do think of Paul as innocent, but I have one particular occasion in mind.

Joanna: What occasion is that?

Barnabas: Perhaps you've heard about Paul's return to Jerusalem from his third missionary journey. His presence in Jerusalem caused some dissension and he was imprisoned by the Romans, partly to protect him, because of trumped up charges that he was a dangerous agitator.

Joanna: Isn't he in Rome now?

Barnabas: Yes, he made it to Rome where he is sharing the good news of our Lord as best as he can while he's under house arrest, but he didn't go there before being in prison for a couple years.

Joanna: If he was imprisoned here and is under house arrest in Rome, why is this an example of his innocence?

Barnabas: Good question, I suppose. Well, Paul is in Rome because he used his prerogative as a Roman citizen to appeal to the emperor.

Joanna: Paul is a Roman citizen?

Barnabas: Yes, he was born in Tarsus, and citizens of Tarsus are also Roman citizens.

Joanna: If he appealed to the emperor, has the emperor declared him innocent?

Barnabas: Not yet, as far as I know. What I meant, though, is that after Paul appealed to the emperor, King Herod Agrippa and Roman Governor Festus both agreed that he was innocent and didn't deserve either death or imprisonment. Paul could have been set free if he hadn't appealed to Caesar.

Joanna: Well, at least his appeal to the emperor got him to Rome.

Barnabas: That's true. Paul long wanted to travel to Rome to preach the good news in the heart of the empire.

Joanna: This all puzzles me.

Barnabas: How so?

Joanna: If Paul was innocent and didn't deserve either death or imprisonment, and if Jesus was both righteous and innocent, then why did they receive death or imprisonment?

Barnabas: That's a good question. I do think it's important for us to emphasize our innocence. We're not really a threat to either the government or religious authorities.

Joanna: I think you're right, but that doesn't really answer my question. If we're so innocent, then why did Jesus and now some of our leaders receive punishment?

Barnabas: It goes back to the beginning of Jesus' ministry. He announced that he came to preach good news to the poor. That may seem innocent enough, but when we begin to show the full extent of God's love for the poor and for others not fully accepted in society, then we may begin to annoy and threaten some people.

Joanna: The righteousness of God means showing compassion to all people, perhaps especially to the poor and lowly. That righteousness may seem innocent, but to leaders it may look like a challenge to their traditions and to their power and authority.

Barnabas: I think that's right. I believe we should keep on insisting on our innocence, even affirming our loyalty to the authorities around us, but also we should always be aware that living out our faith in our Lord may challenge and even threaten those authorities.

Joanna: And, of course, our first loyalty is always to Christ, our Lord.

Barnabas: That's right, but that confession is one of the reasons the empire questions our innocence. We're supposed to confess that the emperor is Lord.

Joanna: I guess they're not content with our being law-abiding people.

Barnabas: No, not to confess the emperor as Lord seems disloyal to them.

Joanna: But we know that Jesus is risen and he is our Lord.

Barnabas: That's the predicament we're in. We don't want to disobey laws and customs, but our faith in Christ gives us no choice except to confess him as Lord and to live by his will.

Joanna: Yes, and that alone may make others question our innocence.

Barnabas: But it doesn't contradict the righteousness we have through following the way of Christ.

Lenten
Commemorations

Polycarp and Ignatius
"You Shall Be Witnesses/Martyrs"
(*Polycarp, bishop of Smyrna, martyr, February 23*)

1 Peter 3:8-16

Narrator: Perpetua, a woman who is a Christian from the city of Ephesus, has made a pilgrimage to Smyrna, the city where Polycarp, recently martyred, had been an honored and beloved bishop. She is talking with Marcion, who just finished writing an account of Polycarp's martyrdom.

Perpetua: It's such an honor for me to meet you. We've heard so much about what a strong and pious Christian Polycarp was and how he remained firm in his faith even as he was led away to be burned. I'm glad someone is writing the story of his death.

Marcion: Thank you, but it is Polycarp, not me, who deserves the honor.

Perpetua: Yes, but telling his story will help others like me understand what it means to be a Christian martyr. Ever since I learned the story of Jesus, I've wondered what he meant when he told his disciples that they would be martyrs.

Marcion: Remember that not all martyrs die for their faith.

Perpetua: But isn't that the ideal? Back in Ephesus we still read the letter that Bishop Ignatius from Antioch wrote to us fifty years ago when he was on his way to Rome to fight with the wild beasts in the arena. He was all excited about going to Rome to "get to God" by suffering like Jesus and dying for his faith. His letter made me feel that dying for our faith is the ultimate way of being a martyr.

Marcion: I wrote about Bishop Polycarp's death because I thought that the way he died made him a martyr for the faith, but he did not seek to die for his faith. No, when he heard that the Romans wanted to kill him, he hid on a farm in the country. When he heard that the Romans were coming to that farm to find him, he hid out on another farm. He said that he was trying to be like Jesus, who didn't seek out the soldiers to arrest him but waited till they came on their own.

Perpetua: Did Polycarp resist the Romans?

Marcion: No, he went with them when they finally found him, but he didn't rejoice in his upcoming death. He faced it with firm faith — bravely but not eagerly. So his way of being a martyr was different than Ignatius' way.

Perpetua: But at least he was a martyr. Some of the Christians in Ephesus say that it doesn't matter if you deny Christ and honor the Roman gods since they don't really exist anyway.

Marcion: They are no martyrs at all, for they are denying their faith in Christ to avoid torture and death.

Perpetua: But how are we supposed to be martyrs and not die?

Marcion: You can be a martyr in your living.

Perpetua: How is that possible?

Marcion: First of all, remember that the basic meaning of "martyr" is to be a witness. You can be a witness for your faith without dying.

Perpetua: Don't you think that the best way to witness is to die for your faith?

Marcion: I do think it is right to honor those who give witness to their faith by dying for it, but I'm not sure that it is the best way. What is best depends on who you are and what happens to you because of your faith.

Perpetua: So we are witnesses by how we live out our faith day by day?

Marcion: Yes, your life can testify to your faith. Have you heard what they are saying about us?

Perpetua: No, what?

Marcion: "See how those Christians love each other." People notice when we follow the way of Christ.

Perpetua: Is that enough to be a martyr? That seems too easy.

Marcion: I don't think so. Showing love to people can take time and work. It can mean finding ways to share food and money with people in need. I'm sure that even in Ephesus you Christians there have many opportunities to reach out with compassion to people within your church community and in the city too.

Perpetua: That's true, and expressing that compassion can be challenging.

Marcion: And showing Christian love is not easy for another reason — some people are pretty difficult to love.

Perpetua: That's for sure. My little brother can be really annoying, and my family, even my father, doesn't support me in my faith in Christ. It is also difficult to love those who want to persecute us believers.

Marcion: It surely is, but just showing love may not be enough. Sometimes martyrs have to speak up. Remember what Peter wrote to us: "Always be ready to give an account of the hope that lies within you."

Perpetua: Talk about my faith in Jesus? I almost think I'd rather face the lions. I'm not as good at words as you or Bishop Polycarp.

Marcion: Your words don't have to be fancy — just an honest expression of your experience of faith. Do you think people might ask you why you came here to Smyrna?

Perpetua: They might. Our neighbors would have noticed that I was gone for a while.

Marcion: Then you could tell people about your trip here and why you came.

Perpetua: I can do that.

Marcion: And if people ask you why you do things to show love to people in need, you can tell them it's because of Jesus and how he showed us God's love for us.

Perpetua: So maybe I can be a martyr while I'm living, both in how I show Christian love in my life and also how I answer questions about my faith.

Marcion: Yes, you can be a living martyr. But I should warn you that testifying through the words and actions of your life can get you into trouble, just like Ignatius and Polycarp.

Perpetua: I can see that, but how can I keep from sharing my faith?

John and Charles Wesley with Susanna Wesley
"A Heart Strangely Warmed"

(John and Charles Wesley, renewers of the Church, March 2)

Ephesians 2:1-10

Narrator: John Wesley is talking with his aged mother Susanna a few years before her death and two years after his famous "Aldersgate Experience," where after hearing a reading of Martin Luther's Preface to Paul's Letter to the Romans his heart was "strangely warmed" by its emphasis on how God can transform us through our faith in Christ, and he was converted to a more personal, emotional piety.

Susanna: My son, I've noticed that lately you seem more joyful somehow.

John: Really? Is it that noticeable?

Susanna: To your mother it is. Was it your experience in that American colony? Which one was it now?

John: Georgia.

Susanna: Yes, that's the one. Was your time there especially joyful?

John: No, it wasn't actually. My attempts to preach the gospel to the colonists and the native Americans weren't very successful, and my preaching against gin and the slave trade wasn't particularly welcome. I was glad to come back home.

Susanna: Well, what is it then?

John: Perhaps it was my experience in Aldersgate a few years ago. I was attending one of my "Methodist" society meetings on Aldersgate Street where I heard someone reading from Martin Luther's Preface to Saint Paul's Letter to the Romans. Luther was going on about how our salvation is a free gift through our faith in Christ, and my heart was "strangely warmed" as I thought about the wonder of God's transforming us freely because of our faith in Christ. From that moment on my method for living my Christian life has been warmed with the joy of knowing God's freely given love in Christ.

Susanna: That's all very nice, but I hope you're not going to get any crazier than you already are.

John: What could be crazy about rejoicing in God's love?

Susanna: Knowing you, my son, I'm sure you can find a way to take your new insight to some extreme. Why couldn't you be more like your brother Charles and write some nice hymns?

(Someone should be heard singing one of Charles Wesley's hymns, like "Hark, the Herald Angels Sing.")

John: I always thought you loved Charles more than me.

Susanna: Now, John, I had too many children to love one more than another. But you two do have different gifts.

John: Yes, we do, but we also share a deep desire to help people deepen their faith in Jesus.

Susanna: You began showing that in your college days at Oxford, didn't you? Charles and you founded that "Holy Society," as I recall.

John: Even then, we thought Christians were too apathetic and interested only in traditional teachings and rituals. We believed we should develop a method of frequent Communion, regular fasting, and helping people in need.

Susanna: "Method," you say. That's when I first started worrying about you going to extremes. Didn't people start calling you "Methodists"?

John: Yes, they did, and they meant that to embarrass us, but I still think it's a good word. Why not have a method to put in practice what Jesus taught us?

Susanna: I guess that's not a bad idea, but won't that make our faith some set of empty habits?

John: I don't think so. Are you implying that religious habits will be empty?

Susanna: I suppose that I am, but haven't you always complained about how dead some of the rituals of the church are?

John: Yes, I have, but I don't think that applies to the habits we include in our method.

Susanna: Why not?

John: Performing certain rituals that have been imposed on you or that you or your family have always done whether they strengthen your faith or not can be dead and empty habits. But developing practices of worship and prayer and service to others that are meaningful and helpful to you would lead to habits that are religiously alive and fulfilling.

Susanna: So you think that your method will lead to a faith that is alive and lively.

John: Yes, I do. We want people to see that faith in Christ is not just going through the motions of worship and speaking the words of some creed. No, faith in Christ is a living and powerful experience that touches people's hearts and empowers them to express their faith in many ways, including trying to meet people's needs.

Susanna: I can see that you are deeply committed to your special "method," and I am beginning to understand why you feel driven to travel all over, even to the colonies, to preach your gospel message and to work for a more just society.

John: I do feel that God has called me to this mission.

Susanna: Interesting, John. I must say that I have been proud of the way that you and Charles have taken your faith seriously, but I hope this "Methodist" business doesn't take you away from our Church of England.

John: I don't plan to leave the Church of England, but practicing genuine personal piety is so important. What good is knowing the joy of God's loving us freely because of Christ if we don't express that faith in our lives? And how better to express it in our lives than by having a method of living out our faith in worship, study, and help for people in need?

Susanna: That is the question — how can we Christians not live lives of personal piety and public service? Oh, there goes your brother again.

(Someone should sing the beginning of another hymn by Charles Wesley.)

A Conversation with Harriet Tubman
"Called to Be Moses"

(Harriet Tubman and Sojourner Truth,
renewers of society, March 10)

Micah 6:1-8

Narrator: The scene tonight is Auburn, New York, the home of Abner Doubleday, the supposed inventor of baseball, but more important for our purposes, also the home of William Seward — New York governor, U.S. senator, and Secretary of State under Presidents Lincoln and Johnson — and the home of Harriet Tubman — a former slave who worked tirelessly to help slaves escape from slavery to freedom in the North. Secretary Seward, also an ardent abolitionist, sold a house to Harriet in Auburn and the city became a haven for escaped African-American slaves before the Civil War. Secretary Seward returned home when Ulysses S. Grant became President in 1869, which is when this conversation took place.

Harriet Tubman: Why, Mr. Seward, it is good to see you back in Auburn again.

William Seward: Thank you, Mrs. Tubman, for saying that! I am glad to be back home and finally to be freed from Washington. How is the house I sold you?

Harriet Tubman: Quite nice, thank you. It surely has served me well, providing me a place to bring my relatives whom I helped to escape from slavery.

William Seward: I'm glad the house has served you so well. I was hoping that selling you the house would help our abolitionist movement.

Harriet Tubman: It was a help to me. You're glad to be free from Washington, but not as happy as the 300 slaves I helped escape to the North — or the 750 I helped free during one of the battles in the Civil War.

William Seward: You were a real "Moses" — freeing the slaves!

Harriet Tubman: That is what some people called me. People also called me "General" because of how I helped in the Civil War. I was the only woman who led an assault in the war. But whatever people called me, what's important, I believe, is that God called me to do this. In my visions God directed me to free slaves.

William Seward: I don't know if I should call you "Moses" or "General Tubman"! What are you doing now that the war is over?

Harriet Tubman: The slaves may be free, but many are poor. I'm raising money for schools for black children. But I'm beginning to think that I should work on freedom for some other folk.

William Seward: What do you mean?

Harriet Tubman: Have you heard about Sojourner Truth?

William Seward: Of course, she's a former slave like you who's been preaching a long time about freeing slaves. She lived for a while in New York but she's in Michigan now, I believe. And doesn't she talk about how God called her to preach against slavery?

Harriet Tubman: Yes, she does. That's why she changed her name to Sojourner Truth. But she's preaching about something else now.

William Seward: She is? What's that? Is there some kind of slavery I'm not aware of?

Harriet Tubman: Perhaps. She's been preaching about equal rights for women. Black men who were slaves can vote now, but women, black or white, still can't vote.

William Seward: Don't tell me you're going to be one of those "suffragettes"!

Harriet Tubman: Well, I surely am. Just as slaves have a right to be free, I believe women have a right to vote. God's calling me to work for their freedom too.

William Seward: But women's place is in the house.

Harriet Tubman: Yes, and in the Senate too!

William Seward: Touché, Mrs. Tubman! I suppose you would add in the governor's mansion and the White House too. I don't know, Mrs. Tubman, this could be quite upsetting.

Harriet Tubman: Yes, it could, but God has always called me to seek freedom and justice for people, even if it was dangerous or risky.

William Seward: Your work to free slaves and even to participate in the Civil War surely was dangerous and risky. I fear that you may continue to see how working for freedom and justice can be dangerous because change is threatening and people in power don't like to be challenged.

Harriet Tubman: I know, but I know God will be with me. I can't stop what I do now.

William Seward: Well, then, you don't think that your work is done.

Harriet Tubman: No, not at all. I believe that God has work for me to do as long as people are suffering from injustice.

William Seward: I imagine that your work will never be done. As long as people pursue power and financial success rather than the common good and compassion for people in need, it will be important to stand up for justice.

Harriet Tubman: Unfortunately, I believe that you are exactly right.

William Seward: Besides your work for freeing slaves, educating their children, and now for women, I wonder who we will need to stand up for.

Harriet Tubman: That's a good question, but whoever is oppressed or whatever injustice there is, I believe we are called by God to "do justice, love kindness, and walk humbly before God."

William Seward: Those are marching orders to keep constant vigilance for where work on justice is needed.

Harriet Tubman: Yes, we need to keep our eyes open to where work on justice and freedom is needed.

William Seward: So God's call didn't stop when slavery was ended.

Harriet Tubman: No, it didn't. There still is much work to do for black folk and for women and for many others too. My visions leave me with another question, "How can I keep from seeking justice for oppressed people?"

Week Four

Saint Patrick
"Connecting with People for the Gospel's Sake"

(*Patrick, bishop, missionary to Ireland, March 17*)

1 Corinthians 9:19-23 and Matthew 28:18-20

Narrator: Tonight's conversation takes place at the Synod of Whitby in Northumbria in seventh-century England. The king of Northumbria followed a form of Christianity based on the Celtic Christianity of Ireland. His queen came from the south of England, whose Christianity derived from the Church in Rome. The Synod of Whitby was called to settle some differences between these two forms of Christianity. The main conflict dealt with how to calculate the date of Easter. The decision of the synod was to follow the procedures of Rome. Our conversation tonight occurs between Sister Fidelma — a member of an Irish religious community and someone trained in Irish law, giving her a function like a district attorney — and Brother Eadulf — a Saxon monk who supported the Church of Rome faction. The Irish law that Sister Fidelma was trained in was codified by a fifth-century commission that included Saint Patrick. The conversation occurs before the synod's final decision.[1]

Brother Eadulf: I don't understand why your Irish party is so stubborn. Our position represents the broad consensus of the whole church. Why don't you just adopt our universal customs?

Sister Fidelma: First of all, your position is not completely universal. Our position is the same as some Eastern Orthodox churches. And secondly, we're not stubborn; we're simply being true to the shape of Christianity that Saint Patrick brought to us.

Brother Eadulf: Is Saint Patrick more important than the Pope?

Sister Fidelma: That question sounds like you're trying to trick me into giving a dangerous answer, but I'm tempted to say "yes," at least for us in Ireland. But remember it was Pope Celestine I who consecrated Patrick as a missionary bishop and sent him to Ireland 200 years ago. Saint Patrick converted our country to Christianity, and we continue to follow what he taught us.

Brother Eadulf: What was so special about him that the Pope sent him to Ireland?

Sister Fidelma: Patrick was born in Britain. Ironically, when he was sixteen, he was kidnapped by some Irish pirates who sold him as a slave. He escaped six years later, but after he returned home he felt a call to convert the Irish to Christianity.

Brother Eadulf: Was he successful in his mission?

Sister Fidelma: Yes, by the time he died Ireland was primarily a Christian country.

Brother Eadulf: Why was he so successful?

Sister Fidelma: Because of the Holy Spirit, of course!

Brother Eadulf: Yes, of course. But what about Saint Patrick did the Spirit use to accomplish the conversion of the Irish people?

Sister Fidelma: Saint Patrick knew the Irish people and their customs and he preached the gospel in ways that respected those customs.

Brother Eadulf: How did he do that?

Sister Fidelma: He understood our tribal system, for example, and worked hard to convert our tribal chieftains so that their people would accept the Christian faith. He developed such trust with our kings and chieftains that he was asked to help develop a code of Irish law — that I'm still trained to use.

Brother Eadulf: His approach seems like simple good sense. Why would it lead to the differences like the ones we're debating here?

Sister Fidelma: Well, in our Irish law women have had many more rights than here in Britain. That's why I can be trained for such a high status legal profession. This has also shaped our church: we have women priests, and some of our monastic communities have both men and women, some of whom are married.

Brother Eadulf: That sounds pretty radical. I wonder if it will last. But are you saying that when we try to share our Christian faith, we need to express it in ways that the people we're talking with can understand and identify with?

Sister Fidelma: Exactly. After all, it was Saint Paul who said that he became all things to all people so that by all means he might save some.

Brother Eadulf: Isn't there a danger that we will distort our Christian faith in order to make it palatable to some unbelieving people?

Sister Fidelma: I think Saint Patrick would agree that this is a risk we need to take. But we do have to be careful.

Brother Eadulf: In what ways do you think we should be careful? Are there limits on the ways we may shape our message to the people we want to reach?

Sister Fidelma: That's a good question, and I don't think there is an easy answer. We must not do or say anything that denies that Jesus is the Son of God who died and rose again for us.

Brother Eadulf: Anything else?

Sister Fidelma: We also must emphasize the grace of God and be sure that people know that God seeks a loving and forgiving relationship with them.

Brother Eadulf: What about morality? Aren't there standards of behavior that all Christians should follow?

Sister Fidelma: Well, the Ten Commandments are a good place to begin, but what precisely it means to love one's neighbor might not be the same in every time and place.

Brother Eadulf: What about loyalty to the church?

Sister Fidelma: That's a tricky one. How the church is structured doesn't always support the basic message we Christians have to preach, and the church can function in different ways and still proclaim what is true in our faith.

Brother Eadulf: Good answers, Sister Fidelma, but what I really want to know is how Saint Patrick drove the snakes out of Ireland.

Sister Fidelma: That's only a legend, Brother Eadulf, but here's a true story, which also illustrates my point — Saint Patrick used one of our plants, the shamrock, to illustrate the doctrine of the Trinity — one plant, three leaves.

Brother Eadulf: Is that why you're wearing green?

Sister Fidelma: In a way. The shamrock has become our national symbol, and it reminds me to share my faith in the Holy Trinity in ways that connect with people. After all, how can I keep from sharing my faith so that others can believe too?

---

1. The occasion of this conversation at the Synod of Whitby is the location of the first of the Sister Fidelma of Cashel mysteries by Peter Tremayne, *Absolution by Murder* (St. Martin's Press, 1995).

Week Five

San Romero
"Justice for the Poor"
(*Oscar Romero, bishop of El Salvador, martyr, March 24*)

Luke 6:20-26

Narrator: Bishop Oscar Romero of El Salvador was assassinated in his cathedral in San Salvador on March 24, 1980, while he was celebrating mass. About ten years later the biographical film "Romero" was released. Our conversation takes place between two people in our country after they saw the film. Mary had visited in El Salvador on a church-sponsored mission trip, but John had not.

Mary: What did you think of the film, John?

John: I found it hard to believe.

Mary: I thought it was quite believable, and it meshed with what I experienced when I was in El Salvador. What seemed unbelievable to you?

John: I can't imagine someone killing a bishop while he's saying mass.

Mary: It was pretty shocking and almost sacrilegious. But why can't you imagine that happening?

John: People just don't risk earning divine displeasure like that. I knew of a priest in our country who refused to let a Mafia boss attend his own daughter's wedding, and no one killed that priest.

Mary: Keeping someone out of church for a wedding is one thing; challenging a ruling regime's system of oppression is another. Just the day before he was killed Bishop Romero preached a sermon criticizing the military for all the killing going on in El Salvador and urging the rank and file peasant soldiers to refuse orders to kill fellow peasants. But, whether you believe it or not, that part of the movie is definitely historical. But I find something else hard to believe in the movie.

John: What's that?

Mary: That Bishop Romero actually stood up and opposed his country's government and military.

John: That apparently was historical too, so why do you find that hard to believe?

Mary: When Bishop Romero first was ordained a priest, he was a timid, pious bookworm who was quite conservative in his theology. When he was consecrated a bishop, people who were concerned about the plight of the poor in El Salvador were very disappointed. The church establishment tended to side with the ruling government and wealthy landowners, and no one expected that Bishop Romero would change that.

John: What happened to change him?

Mary: Shortly after he was consecrated as El Salvador's archbishop, his first priest and two of his parishioners were killed, apparently shot by a government death squad. Bishop Romero realized that if they could kill his priest friend, who was working with poor peasants, he was vulnerable too.

John: Weren't those priests who were working with the peasants all Marxists?

Mary: Maybe some of them were, but most were influenced by "liberation theology."

John: What's that? Isn't that just a cover for Communist ideology?

Mary: Oh, no! "Liberation theology" began with the Exodus and emphasized God's actions to free people from slavery and oppression.

John: But the Exodus was a one-time event in history. Isn't that a misuse of scripture to apply it to current events?

Mary: You might disagree with applying the Exodus event to some current situation, but it's hardly a misuse of scripture. Even in the Bible what happened in the Exodus is frequently applied to other times in history. Isaiah talks about the Jews' return from exile in Babylon as if it were a new Exodus.

John: But that's in the Old Testament, not the New Testament.

Mary: Yes, but those Hebrew scriptures are part of our Bible too, and in his gospel Luke talks about Jesus' journey to Jerusalem as being a kind of Exodus. Besides, the priests influenced by liberation theology interpreted the resurrection as opening the door to a new life of freedom and justice, especially for poor people.

John: Doesn't that just interject a political agenda into the Bible?

Mary: Concern for justice for the poor doesn't interject anything into the Bible, although there may be different political ways to accomplish it. No, justice for the poor is a concern that runs throughout the Bible. If you cut out all the passages in the Bible that command believers to care for the poor and for the widow and the orphan, there wouldn't be very much of the Bible left.

John: Doesn't the Bible also command obedience to government?

Mary: Yes, it does, although those passages are few in comparison, and there are many, many more passages where the prophets criticize government leaders for their neglecting the poor. And the Bible also says that we are to obey God rather than humans.

John: Are you saying that as Christians we should be concerned about justice for the poor?

Mary: Yes!

John: Do we have to care about places like El Salvador?

Mary: I think so. Maybe we can't do much for every place where there is injustice, but our world is more and more interconnected. The mission trip I was on helped me to understand the situation in another country, and it was a way for our group to help a little bit. We can also encourage our government to do things to promote freedom and justice. But there are plenty of reasons to be concerned about justice right in our own country.

John: Do you really think so? We're a free country with liberty and justice for all.

Mary: That's our ideal and mostly we live up to it, but I think we can still find injustice if we look carefully. Look at the hunger and homelessness around us. I think there are issues of justice that lead to some of the needs we have in our country. So I definitely think that we Christians have reasons to be concerned about justice for the poor.

John: But doesn't the example of Bishop Romero show how dangerous that can be?

Mary: It can be dangerous, but I would hope it would not be that dangerous for us. But like Bishop Romero, we might feel that we have no alternative — our faith calls us to seek God's justice whatever the cost.

John: That's definitely a challenge — big-time.

Mary: Yes, but how can I keep from seeking God's will for justice for the poor?